Journey through

# GERMANY

Photos by

Horst and Daniel Zielske,

Martin Siepmann

and Karl-Heinz Raach

Text by

Ernst-Otto Luthardt

Stürtz

# CONTENTS

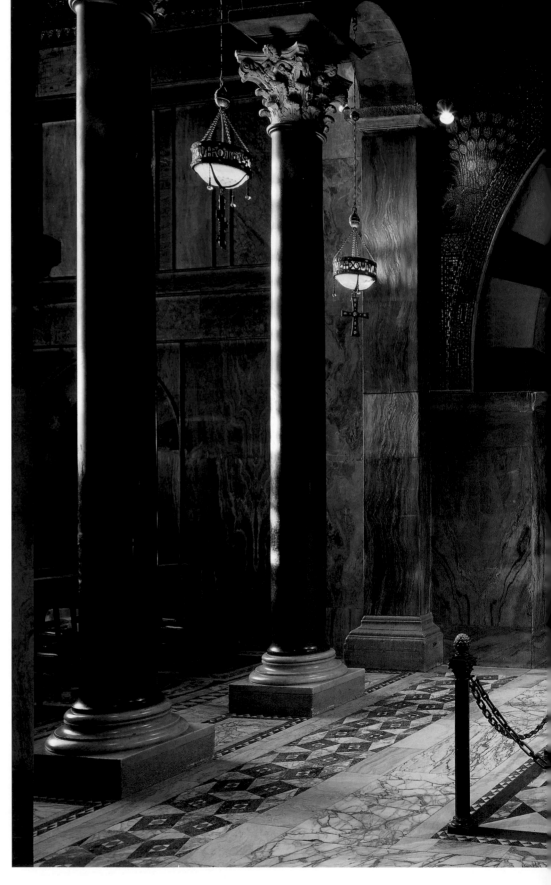

*The Palatine chapel at the heart of Aachen's minster was built by Charlemagne between 786 and 805. This is where 30 German kings and emperors were crowned between the 10th and 16th centuries. The emperor's marble throne has six steps going up to it, like that of King Solomon.*

Of all the crowned heads in medieval Europe it was the kings of Germany whose thirst for travel was the most insatiable. They forged east, hungry for new domains and rich booty, and down into Italy. From 962 onwards they successfully swelled the territories of the Kingdom of Germany in the Holy Roman Empire – and increasingly neglected their duties at home. The fall of the Staufer dynasty in 1254 signalled the end of a centralised regal power, making way for the ascension of the more prosperous towns and of territorial sovereigns both sacred and secular. Each made politics as they thought fit, seeing themselves as big-time potentates with the power to rule. The many royal capitals blossomed and built theatres with orchestras to play in them. Local magnates collected valuable works of art and beautiful female artistes; they constructed one splendid edifice after another until the coffers were empty. The wealthy free cities were every bit as ambitious as their princely cousins.

# WOULD BE KING

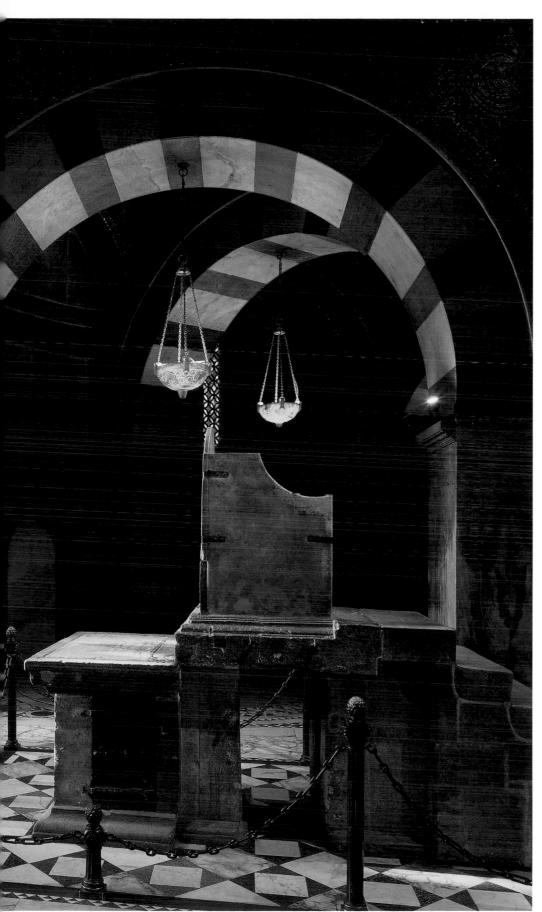

As paradox as it may seem, it's this period of political fiasco which has left Germany with the rich architectural and cultural legacy tourists today find so compelling.

## WHERE THE LAND MEETS THE SEA

In the Middle Ages, when the sea was thought to be the beginning of the end of the world, the marine merchants who formed the Hanseatic League made it their objective to venture out to new shores and sources of profit. The largest of Germany's confederation of cities which flourished in the 14th century successfully seized control of trade on the northern seas and prospered. Lübeck, Hamburg, Bremen and the remaining members of the League proudly exhibited their new-found wealth, having ornate houses, hospitals, town halls and churches erected in legendary Gothic brick.

Schleswig-Holstein was initially a province of seafarers and farmers. This changed when the discovery was made that the sea is a marketable commodity. The tourist industry boomed. It now attaches greater value to holidays with class as opposed to those en masse; modern-day strand-lovers have enough opportunities to escape the obligatory seaside attractions of the more sizeable beaches. There are desert islands for would-be Robinson Crusoes for hire – at least for the duration of a holiday – in both North and East Frisia.

The East Frisian holiday isles of Norderney, Borkum and Spiekeroog belong to not to Schleswig-Holstein but to Lower Saxony. The second-largest German province stretches from the low mountains of the Harz to the beautiful briny North Sea. The land in between is flat but far from boring. Take the superb heathlands around Lüneburg, for example, whose carpet of heather swathes the nature reserve in brilliant cerise in the autumn. Or the castles and town houses of the Weser Renaissance, whose richly ornamented stone and half-timbered façades have many a mysterious tale to tell.

## THE STATES THAT ARE CITIES

Before the River Weser runs into the North Sea, it weaves its way through an ancient city whose foundation goes back to 787 and a bishopric established by Emperor Charlemagne. In the 11th century Bremen was thus known as the Rome of the North, until three centuries later the city's development fell to the minds and monies of the Hansas. This period of prosperity is preserved in stone on the market place, for example, with the cathedral, Schüttinghaus and town hall – not forgetting the stone giant called Roland, who has guarded the city's privileges with his sword and shield since 1404.

Like Berlin and Hamburg, Bremen is both city and federal state. With Bremerhaven as its coastal port, Bremen covers an area of around 155 square miles (400 square kilometres) and is the smallest of Germany's provinces.

Almost twice this size, but still minuscule compared to Lower Saxony in which both city states lie, is Hamburg, which has Germany's biggest harbour. The world's largest loading zone with its northern docklands has a strong pull on tourists. Not only are the halls and warehouses good for business – so are the façades, which imitate the Hansas in neo-Gothic. Unlike some of the other communes in the League, Hamburg's importance and magnetism is due to both the past and the present. At almost two million inhabitants, the metropolis isn't just a top international address for commerce and industry but also for art and theatre, opera and ballet. It also boasts a famous entertainment centre in the St Pauli district.

## CRAMPED CONDITIONS AND MARCHING BANDS

The people in North Rhine-Westphalia (18 million) live in the fourth largest of the federal states. Conditions are particularly cramped for both man and machine in the industrial Ruhr area, Europe's vastest conurbation, where municipalities such as Bochum, Gelsenkirchen, Leverkusen and Recklinghausen have long swallowed any no-man's land which may have existed

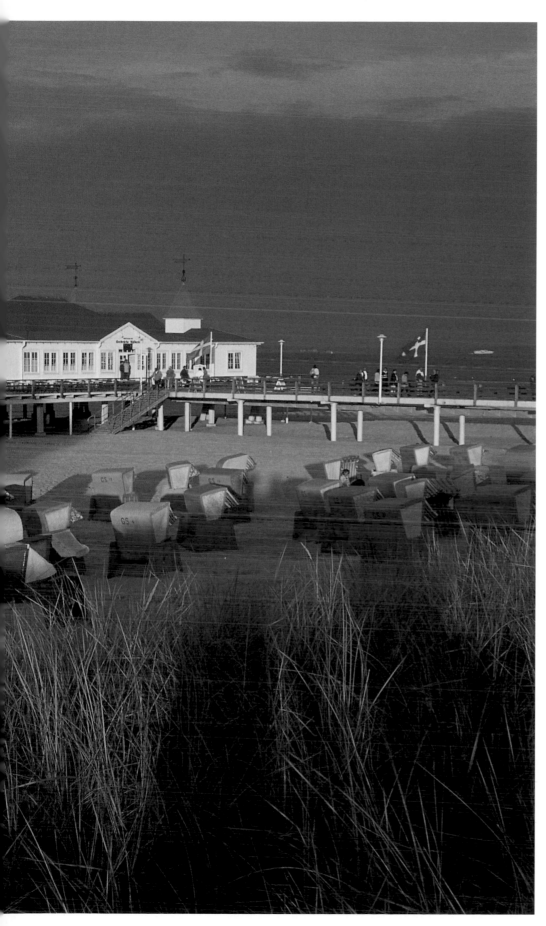

between them. Yet each year at Carnival time people happily hurl themselves into the throng. They swamp the dance halls in their masks and costumes and jig through the streets to the beat of marching bands and processional floats on Rosenmontag. The best parades are in Cologne or Düsseldorf. While we're on the subject: Cologne on the River Rhine was the biggest Roman settlement north of the Alps, with the springs at Aachen providing hours of imperial fun at the baths. The Carolingian to Gothic cathedrals in the two cities look back on a great German imperial and architectural history. Yet North Rhine-Westphalia isn't all industry and urbanity. In the volcanic northern Eifel and Sauerland, where world championships in bob sport and tobogganing are held, it also has some fine countryside.

## WHERE WITCHES DANCE

Once the Saxon rulers had been crowned kings they were drawn east to convert the heathen slaves and confiscate their land. The stone witnesses to this period line the Romantic Route as churches and castles. In Quedlinburg Prince Heinrich was pursuing his favourite pastime of catching finches in 919 when news reached him that he had been elected king of Germany. His final resting place in the collegiate church atop the castle hill is one of the grand legacies of Romanesque art in Germany, as is the church of St Cyriakus in Gernrode.

Back to the Harz. Its highest peak, the Brocken, is serviced by a particularly romantic railway line, along which chugs an aged steam train. A quicker mode of transport is undoubtedly the broomstick the witches from near and far are said to use on Walpurgis Night (30 April). This is when they fly up what has been Germany's witch mountain since the Middle Ages to their cackling equivalent of a rave.

## BY BOAT TO THE REINSTATED CAPITAL

In Mecklenburg-West Pomerania it's not witches you're likely to come across, but giants. Tales of prehistoric ogres and phantom sea monsters have survived to our present day, as have more tangible relics of the past: little fishing villages with thatched roofs, unspoilt scenery, like that of the Darß, and seaside resorts which over the decades have transmuted from splendour to shabbiness. Now the coastal architecture of places such as Heringsdorf, Kühlungsborn and Ahlbeck in stone and wood once again basks in its former glory. One particularly charming location is Rügen, Germany's largest island, where precipitous cliffs of gleaming chalk are interspersed with flat, sandy beaches. This is the province where the Baltic has an inland counterpart, smaller maybe but no less idyllic. The Mecklenburg Seenplatte or lake district is a refuge for many protected species of animal and plant. Hobby sailors can glide along the lakes, rivers and canals to and beyond Berlin.

In 1991, Germany's biggest community once again became capital city and heart of a reunified nation. Berlin is also the country's chief building site. The modern age, with its flash ministries, company headquarters and cultural centres, is rapidly engulfing both east and west of a city once divided. Friedrichstraße, for example, has been given a completely new visage.

Besides the better-known architectural highlights (Schloss Charlottenburg, for example, at the pinnacle of Prussian design) and ark of museums (the most famous being museum island with its top-class exhibits from the world of international art), the standard itinerary should include an excursion to the real Berlin, to soak up the atmosphere in the authentic pubs, galleries and theatres in Prenzlauer Berg, for example – with the people to match. For the more contemplative (and solitary) moments there are the lakes and pine forests of Brandenburg which encircle the city centre. In defiance of the old saying, here the Prussians built upon sandy ground. Frederick the Great, who loved war and hated women, is the embodiment of the Prussians' surprising rise to European power. In Schloss Sanssouci he has bequeathed to the world a place of enchantment which refuses to gel with the Prussian notion of prudence.

## THE LAND OF CHRISTMAS

For many centuries the Saxons were the Prussians' strongest adversaries. Their capital Dresden flowered into the Florence of the River Elbe. Art and literature were promoted, their composers famous all over Europe. The legend of J.S. Bach lives on not just in his music but also in the Choir of St Thomas's in Leipzig. Bach was from Thuringia, which at that time belonged to Saxony and still has much in common with its neighbour. The old heartland of Luther's Reformation is endowed with a variety of beautiful countryside and a healthy architectural and spiritual heritage. The provincial capital of Thuringia, Erfurt, is one of the most historically interesting cities in Germany. Yet it's not a mutual past alone which continues to link the two federal states. They also share a long tradition which is still very much alive – the manufacture of Christmas goods. In Thuringia fascinated visitors purchase hand-blown baubles for their Christmas trees before moving on to Saxony's Erzgebirge, which with its abundance of candle-powered pyramids, wooden figures and nutcrackers, old customs and seasonal fêtes is the land of Christmas.

## THE BEAUTIFUL LORELEY

You would think that with the vast number of industrial plants clogging its banks, Germany's largest river, the Rhine, must by now resemble a sewer. Not so. The song warbled by visitors to this famous wine country, which opens "If the water in the Rhine were golden wine...", thus doesn't seem as unappetising as it might first appear. In Hesse indeed, where the dense forests are the stuff fairy tales are made of, it isn't that implausible to hope that one day this dream might come true. The state even has a German Fairy-Tale Route which links up the age-old stories and little towns and leads to the castle of Sleeping Beauty, the Sababurg. There are just as many fortresses and homely half-timbered villages lining a second, equally famous road, the Bergstraße. This is at its most magical in spring, when the fruit trees smother the slopes in white.

Another legend concerns a beautiful maiden who used to sit on the steep rocks above the River Rhine and sing so enchantingly that the sailors below fell into a trance and perished in the swirling waters. Although the lady in question hasn't been seen for some time, nor has her song been heard, the magnetism of her alleged haunt is stronger than ever before. The Loreley Rock is one of the most popular places of yearning in the whole of Germany. The Rhine is indeed at its best between Mainz and Koblenz, with batteries of castles, vineyards and romantic villages. It thus comes as no great surprise that this bit of paradise on earth was so well-loved by the rulers of the Kingdom of Germany in the Holy Roman Empire that they wished to stay here even after death. The cathedral in Speyer has no less than eight German emperors and kings laid to rest in its vaults. The Romanesque cathedrals of the provincial capital Mainz and in Worms, the old abbey at Maria Laach and many other churches here powerfully mirror the

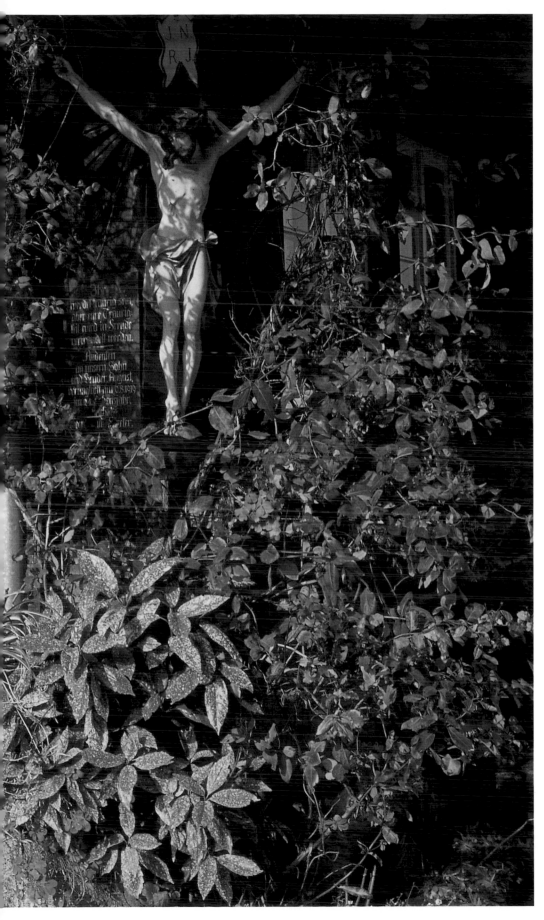

thoughts and emotions of a bygone age. The oldest city in Germany is thought to be Trier, founded over 2,000 years ago by the Romans and in 285 chosen as the capital of the western reaches of their empire.

From Trier it's a stone's throw to the Saarland. For years this area was a political bone of contention for »arch enemies« France and Germany. It only became a more permanent part of Germany in 1957 by way of a plebiscite. The people here not only have an iron, steel and engineering industry which once held great significance for the area; into this nation between nations they have injected a strong dose of French savoir-vivre which has not only relaxed relations between the two countries but has also enriched the Saarland cuisine. Here there are restaurants which are so good you can spare yourself the trip to France.

The region was never a holiday resort in the classical sense of the word. Yet despite the former predominance of the coal and steel industry nature has managed to reserve a place for itself, such as in the impressive bend in the River Saar near Mettlach. And following the end of the local »iron age«, or rather an economic restructuring, many of the industrial strongholds have undergone a wonderful transformation, those in Saarlouis, Neukirchen, Völklingen and elsewhere now home to museums or arts centres.

## THE CAPITAL OF ROMANTICISM

In the romantic capital of Heidelberg there's a danger, according to a famous song, of losing your heart. Others see a greater threat of cardiac injury in the Black Forest. This range of low mountains, with its ancient pine forests and pretty villages, has earned itself a reputation as the almost perfect holiday destination. Even today things here are a bit different, the pace of life more leisurely and humane. Time hides in the wooden Black Forest clocks, waiting for the little door to open and a cuckoo to betray its whereabouts. Yet life in Baden-Württemberg can be led in the fast line; after all, this is where cars by Mercedes and Porsche are made. And where on Lake Constance scientists dabble in supersonic space technology.

## A FESTIVAL TO BEAT ALL FESTIVALS

In Bavaria people don't always walk about in Lederhosen and dirndls as the ads would have us believe. Yet at the Oktoberfest in Munich you're quite likely to find yourself surrounded by people sporting traditional dress – and drinking full-bodied beer to which the obligatory Weißwurst sausages must be consumed. The biggest public festival in the world takes on an added dimension by being staged in Munich. Its metropolitan flair is a mixture of Alpine joie de vivre, up-to-the-minute modernism and trend-setting chic. If you come to the Oktoberfest without looking round Munich, you'll have missed out. The same goes for Germany's city of dreams, Rothenburg ob der Tauber in Bavarian Franconia. It has survived since the Middle Ages unscathed, a greeting from another world.

Franconia was also the domain of the great German artists of the late Gothic and Renaissance. Among them were sculptor Veit Stoß and painter Albrecht Dürer, whose work and lives are inextricably linked to the imperial free city of Nuremberg. The altars and carvings of Tilman Riemenschneider, on the other hand, can be found both in and around Würzburg and in the delightful valley of the Tauber. Goethe for one was a particular fan of this archaic cultural landscape. He bought books, maps, coins and porcelain for his collections from Nuremberg and wine from Würzburg. And had Maria in his famous play »Götz von Berlichingen« knowingly proclaim: »Franconia is a divine land!«

*The lush, rolling hills of the Allgäu run from Lake Constance in the west to the River Lech in the east, with picturesque villages, historic towns and fairy-tale castles forming a glorious prelude to the peaked ranges of the Alps. Here, the view from Ussenburg of Rieden, the Forggensee, the Schwangau and Säuling.*

*Page 22/23:*
*The white chalk cliffs on the Baltic island of Rügen plunge straight* down into the sea. Romantic artists and poets saw in them a sparkling white wedding dress for the union of sky and water, the ancient trees a nuptial bouquet in green.

What kind of people choose to set up home in the middle of the mudflats of the North Sea? On tiny islands, whose names – Nordstrandischmoor and Nordmarsch-Langeneß-Blutwehl – seem longer than the isles themselves. And where these flat, tiny strips of land are at such risk that buildings are erected on artificial hills, their inhabitants living on stilts.

It's said that a landscape moulds the people who live in it and vice versa. The inhabitants of Northern Germany, for example, are known as „fish heads", not in reference to their appearance but to their temperament. In difficult situations their motto is to wait and see, or, as they put it, to „wait and drink tea". They then roll up their sleeves and set to with a vengeance.

Over 100 years ago a tiny village in the moors around Bremen made art history. In Worpswede, painters such as H. Mackensen, H. Vogeler and P. Modersohn began exploring new avenues of artistic expression. They recreated the land and its people on canvas.

What the palette and paintbrush were to Worpswede, coal and ore were to the River Ruhr. The ground was turned into a giant Swiss cheese. The locals squeezed their homes in between enormous winding towers and factory buildings; work and leisure couldn't have been more closely interwoven. The giants of industry dwarfed the modest abodes of their employees, who furnished their houses with pride and panache, with miniature paradise gardens, with pigeon lofts and rabbit hutches in the shed. Life here has since changed but the local dialect remains in testimony to the past. The local word for miner is still used to describe anyone who's a friend or Kumpel.

**Page 28/29:**
*Landing stages at St Pauli. Acting as a bridge between the river and the open sea, these huge two-storey „water stations", almost 2,300 ft/700 m long, float on giant pontoons.*

**Below:**
*About every 10th job in the Hanseatic city of Hamburg is in some way still linked to the harbour, whose origins go back to the 12th century. The „gateway to the world" is almost 33 square miles (85 square kilometres) in size.*

**Right and centre right:**
*Hamburg's container depot is among the top six in the world. Its state-of-the-art warehouses form a futuristic contrast to the Speicherstadt, erected in true Historicist style at the middle of the 19th century (centre right).*

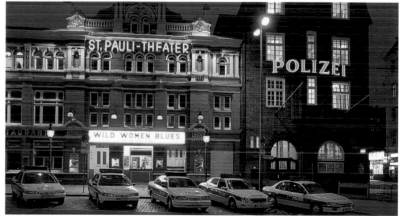

**Below and centre:**
Originally set up for Hamburg's seafaring travellers, the red-light Reeperbahn has long been a centre of entertainment for sailors and landlubbers alike. The street name Große Freiheit ("great freedom") is a reminder of the privileges of 1611/12, to which the district of Altona owes its rise to prosperity. The Davidwache at the corner of Davidstraße and Reeperbahn is probably the most famous police station in Germany, having had a starring role in a large number of films.

**Top:**
Minus its Köhlbrandbrücke, a daring, giddy construction 1,640 ft (500 m) in length which links the harbour to the hinterland, Hamburg traffic would come to a standstill. The bridge across the Süderelbe was built in 1973/74.

**Below:**
Once a commonplace affair, later relegated to the open-air museum, thatched roofs are coming back into fashion. Houses covered in this natural material aren't just for romantics; thatch also has a number of practical advantages.

**Right:**
As the name would suggest, the „elbow" is a narrow, curved peninsula which juts out into the sea at the northern end of Sylt. The sand dunes surrounding the „Hook of East India" are listed.

**Top right:**
In St Peter Ording the beach is over 6 miles (10 km) long and in places almost 1,640 ft (500 m) wide. The North Frisian spa on the tip of the Eiderstedt peninsula is known far and wide for its unusual local sport: beach sailing.

**Centre right:**
Travemünde is one of the oldest, largest and most famous Baltic towns in Germany. Details of its 19th-century history and various anecdotes have been worked in the Thomas Mann novel „Buddenbrooks". The beach today is around 3 miles (5 km) long.

**Bottom right:**
List is one of the seven resorts on Sylt, the largest and chicest of the North Frisian islands (38 square miles/100 square kilometres in surface area). Sylt's beauty lies not only in its beaches but also in its fabulous dunes, in the steep coastline of the „red cliff" and in the tranquil moorland encircling the villages inland.

In the mudflats of Lower Saxony near Sahlenburg. This unique area of beach, which changes with the tides, was made a national park in 1986. Guided walks introduce you to the many amphibious life-forms which exist here.

*Until 1915, the lighthouse on top of the Pilsum dyke
helped helmsmen navigate their ships safely into the
Dollart from the Osterems and Westerems. Now an
East Frisian landmark, the disused tower is painted
red and yellow instead of the usual red and white.*

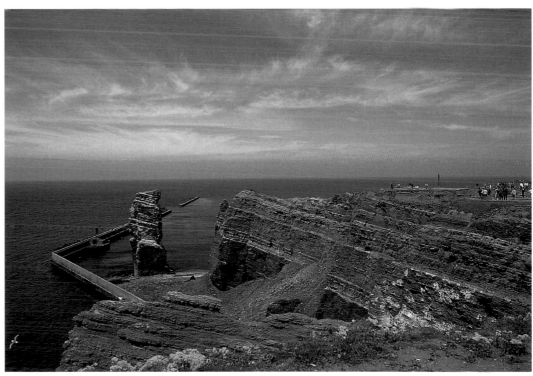

*Helgoland, a crag island in the North Sea, is not even
a third of a square mile (a square kilometre) in size,
yet is a great tourist magnet. The coastal path along
the top of the cliffs enables visitors to study the*

*bizarre rock formations from above. „Lange Anna",
a free-standing obelisk formed by the sea, is the
symbol of the island and under a conservation order.*

Kiel and its many
visitors from all over the
world have taken part in
the Kieler Woche sailing
regatta on the Baltic Sea

each June since 1882.
The sporting activities
are paralleled by an
extremely varied pro-
gramme of top-class cul-

tural events, turning
the Kieler Woche into a
summer festival of inter-
national calibre.

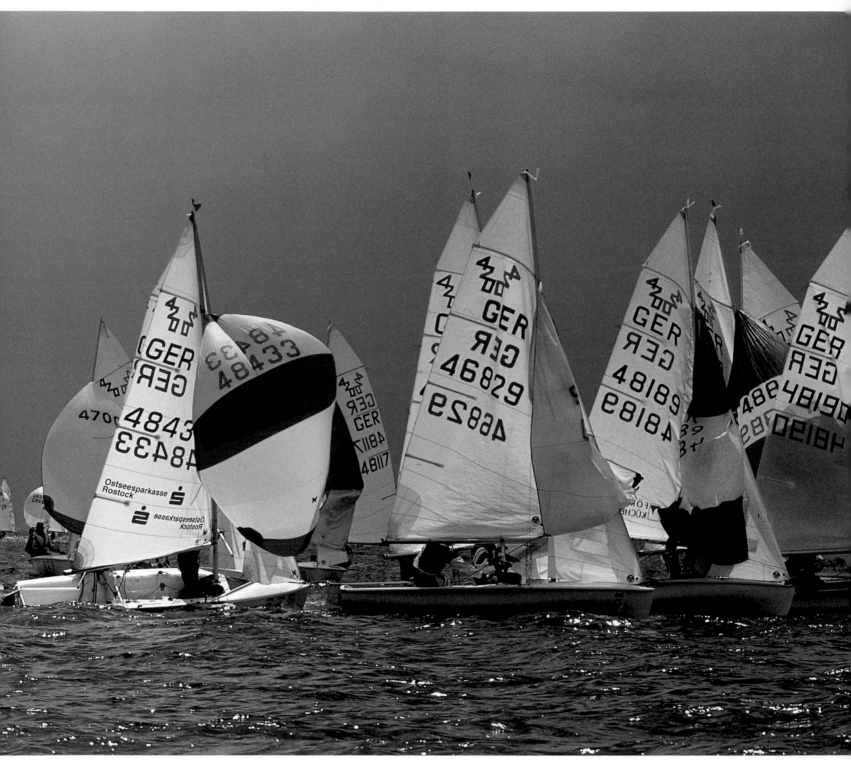

In keeping with Kiel's
long tradition of regattas,
in 1936 and 1972 the
provincial capital of
Schleswig-Holstein was
asked to host the
Olympic sailing contest.
Incidentally, there are
plenty of yachts and
sailing boats to see here
all year round.

Kiel's greatest advantage
lies in its location on the
heavily trafficked Kiel
Canal. The town itself is
said to „look to the north",
a not unapt prognosis;
Oslo- and Schweden-Kai
are important stepping
stones to Scandinavia.

**Above:**
With its many old houses from the Gothic brick and Renaissance periods, Lübeck, once the „queen of the Hansas", is one of Germany's most interesting cities. The above photo shows the Holstenhaven, around which merchant's residences and storehouses parade their splendid gables.

**Above right:**
The irrefutable landmark of Lübeck, founded by Henry the Lion, is the 16th-century Holstentor. So many of the bricks were laid incorrectly when the gateway was built that it has subsided and now leans slightly to one side.

**Bottom right:**
The Viking settlement of Haithabu dates back to the 9th century and even had its own mint. The remains of the site have been excavated and partly reconstructed, producing many finds which are on display here at the museum. The absolute highlight is the magnificent Viking longboat.

**Top left:**
*The cathedral in Ratzeburg towers majestically above the town and harbour. The famous building, pre-Lübeck, demonstrates how simple bricks can be put to monumental use. The outstanding Romanesque edifice goes back to the duke of Lower Saxony, Henry the Lion, for whom Ratzeburg was his last place of refuge before he was banished to England in 1181.*

**Bottom left:**
*The island of Fehmarn can boast two super latives; it's not only the sunniest area in Germany, but also the one with the least rainfall. Among the 42 villages is Orth in the west of the island, shown here with its harbour.*

**Below:**
*Affluence came to the old port of Flensburg through its trade with the West Indies. The town experienced a boom from 1440 to 1867, when it was under Danish rule.*

**Page 40/41:**
*Bremen's market place, seen at its best. The huge stone figure of Roland (1404) symbolises urban independence from the rule of the archbishops.*

# JOHANN WOLFGANG VON GOETHE

On November 7 1775 Goethe arrived in Weimar – and caused something of a sensation. Or rather, his clothes did. He was dressed like a parrot in his blue-and-yellow Werther suit, sported by the hero of his epistolary novel „The Sorrows of Young Werther" published the previous year. Far from disclaiming the autobiographical nature of his book, the author openly admitted to it, later saying that he let his unhappy, lovelorn protagonist die so that he could continue living.

Although Goethe had received a personal invitation to Weimar from 18-year-old Duke Karl August himself, to the courtiers and citizens of the minuscule royal capital he was the man they loved to hate. Bringing the bard to Weimar was, in their opinion, simply asking for trouble! Supposedly acting as chief educator to the prince, Goethe turned out to be wilder than the regent himself. One

winter the young duke and his mentor strapped wooden ice skates to their shoes and skidded about on the flooded, frozen meadows along the River Ilm, spending more of their time prostrate than upright, much to the scandalised amusement of hundreds of onlookers.

Luckily for Goethe, he not only managed to curry favour with Karl August but also with a more mature, extremely influential member of the court, Charlotte von Stein. It's to her that credit must undoubtedly go for forming the Stürm-und-Drang poet in such a way that Weimar became not just an episode but the main chapter in his life.

Besides his antics at court, the „young wild one" also dabbled in politics. He quickly found himself elected to join the Secret Council, Weimar's government. Starting out as a mere counsellor to a legation of the council, the pinnacle of his political career was as the highest servant to the duchy – as head of government.

His interests and hobbies were unbelievably manifold and interwoven. Not only did he make big politics in the little city of Weimar, introducing one top play after another to the stage; he was also a successful scientist. He discovered the intermaxillary bone in humans, published a „Theory of Colour" and made various other important contributions on geological and biological topics. Unlike many, he was capable of being productive in a number of diverse fields – and in many cases also proved himself a pioneer.

Goethe was naturally a very different character from Schiller. The latter wasn't invited to Weimar, but came to be near the man he admired in the hope that his idol might help and support him. Which he indeed did. 1794 marked the beginning of a close friendship between the two greats of German literature. Following a period as a history lecturer in Jena, Schiller settled in Weimar permanently in 1799. He and Goethe often met, discussed various subjects, got worked up about the same things and competed with each other with their plays. Their main venue was the theatre in Weimar, of which Goethe was director until 1816. He walked out when one of the duke's actress mistresses brought a trained dog onto stage to take on the main role.

Unlike Goethe, Schiller, who was plagued by constant ill health and financial worry, couldn't allow himself such affronts. He had to take whatever work came his way.

**Far left:**
*The garden house on the River Ilm was one of young Goethe's favourite places.*

**Left:**
*Goethe's study in his house on Frauenplan in Weimar. The poet wrote standing up at his desk.*

In 1804, for example, when hereditary prince Karl Friedrich married Anna Pavlovna, daughter of the tsar of Russia, Goethe was first asked to pen an ode to the happy couple. Only when he refused was Schiller asked if he would compose a suitable piece.

Schiller's difficulties in Weimar didn't end with his death. He succumbed to a serious lung infliction on May 9 1805, but was buried three days later, one hour after midnight, at the cemetery of St Jacob's, in a communal tomb reserved for those who had no family grave of their own.

A good two decades later, when 23 skulls were excavated from the vault, the largest was identified as being that of Schiller's. The mortal remains of Friedrich von Schiller and Johann Wolfgang von Goethe now rest in peace in the royal vault of Weimar's „new" cemetery.

*Bottom:*
*The statue of Goethe and Schiller in front of Weimar's national theatre was created by famous Saxon sculptor Ernst Rietschel in 1857.*

*Above:*
*The Schiller National-museum in Marbach on the Neckar River fondly commemorates the town's greatest personality.*

## Johann Wolfgang von Goethe

Born on 28.8.1749 in Frankfurt am Main.
Studies law in Leipzig, Frankfurt and Straßburg (1770). Meets Herder and other poets associated with the Sturm und Drang movement.
Returns to Frankfurt and produces his first literary work. Achieves instant fame in Germany with his novel „The Sorrows of Young Werther" (1774).
1775: moves to Weimar at the invitation of Grand Duke Carl August. Soon becomes involved in all major affairs of government.
1786–1788: travels to Italy to escape the restrictions of the court in Weimar.
1788: meets Schiller for the first time.
1790: „Urfaust" is published.
1791–1816: director of the theatre in Weimar.
1806: marries Christiane Vulpius, with whom he has already lived for many years, an employee at a paper flower manufacturer's.
1807–1833: publication of his autobiography „Of my Life. Poetry and Truth". Dies on 22.3.1832.

## Friedrich von Schiller

Born on 10.11.1759 in Marbach (Neckar).
1773–1780: studies law, then from 1775 on medicine at the Karlsschule in Württemberg.
1782: following the premier of his play „The Robbers" the name of the young regimental doctor is on every-one's lips. Schiller seizes the opportunity to desert.
1789: professor of history in Jena, a post arranged by Goethe in order to secure Schiller's financial situation.
1790: marries Charlotte von Legenfeld, daughter of an army officer from Rudolstadt in Thuringia.
From 1791 onwards: his tuberculosis gradually wor-sens.
From 1794 onwards: works with his friend Goethe on literary theories and various ballads.
1799: finally settles permanently in Weimar.
Dies on 9.5.1805. Schiller's most famous works the world over are his plays (the „Wallenstein" trilogy, „Wilhelm Tell" and „Maria Stuart").

Hanover, once the royal seat of the Welf dynasty (1636–1866), was granted its town charter in the 13th century. It was made the provincial capital of Lower Saxony in 1946. The fate of the community of 500,000 is determined at the Neues Rathaus on Maschteich. Much of the town's historic core was destroyed in the Second World War, allowing a more generous layout of the post-war buildings which replaced them.

One of Hanover's greatest attractions is the baroque *Großer Garten* in Herrenhausen. Among the guests of electoral princess Sophie (1630–1714) to stay at the palace were philosopher Leibniz and composer Handel.

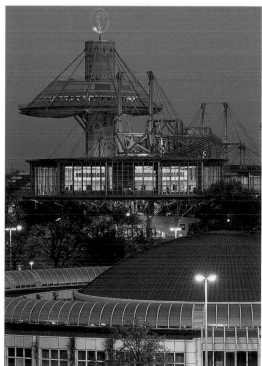

**Above:**

Wolfsburg is home to a strange combination: Volkswagen cars and the muses. The architecture of the art museum (1994) is as interesting as its contents. The glass canopy which spans the individual sections of the building seems to rest weightlessly on 18 slim pillars.

**Left:**

View of the conference hall at the Hanover trade fair, one of the largest major centres of business in the world. It not only attracts managers and bankers, but also many interested visitors.

45

The Elbe, Germany's second-largest river, rises in the Bohemian mountains and flows into the North Sea at Cuxhaven. It changes frequently along its course, shaping the countryside and the lives of the people it passes on its journey. Here the river runs through the flatlands of northern Germany.

Sand, fine grass, juniper bushes, flocks of sheep and lonely farmsteads are the melancholy trademarks of the Lüneburg Heath between Hanover and Hamburg. The area was once covered in dense forest, felled to provide fuel for the fires saltmakers kept burning under their extraction pans. The heath could thus be said to be the work of man.

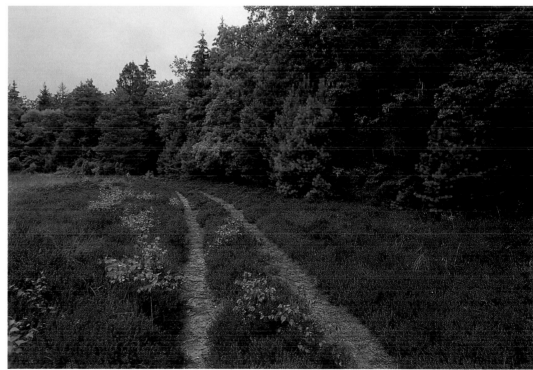

In bad weather or at dusk the heathlands seem eerie and almost threatening, making them a popular setting for tales of ghosts and murder. In the summer, however, when the heather is in full flower, glistening in the bright sunshine, the heath glows crimson.

47

**Below:**
Celle, on the southern edge of the Lüneburg Heath, is one of the old towns in Lower Saxony whose half-timbered buildings have been wonderfully preserved. The old town was laid out in the 14th century and extended in the 16th; the fine gabled house fronts all look out onto the street.

**Right:**
The cathedral at Hildesheim was founded in 872. Badly damaged during the Second World War, it was quickly restored to its former glory. Its Ottonian and Romanesque furnishings and the cathedral treasure are among the most valuable surviving works of medieval sacred art in Germany.

**Left:**
*In the mid-12th century Stade was given the right to hold a market and a court of law and also to mint coins and levy tolls. A member of the Hanseatic League, it was the centre of maritime trade for southern Lower Saxony and the main market town in the Lower Elbe region.*

**Below:**
*To traveller Alexander von Humboldt, that Hannoversch-Münden was one of the most magnificently situated towns in the world. Located at the confluence of the Werra and Fulda rivers, the half-timbered array of the historic Altstadt takes some beating.*

**Below centre:**
*Lüneburg, an old Hanseatic town, lies on the northern reaches of the heath which bears its name. Unlike many of its northern German counterparts, Lüneburg has managed to retain its medieval appearance. One of the marvellous town churches is the Johanniskirche.*

**Above:**
*Barkenhoff in Worpswede belonged to painter Heinrich Vogeler, who at the turn of the 19th century, gathering friends and like-minded individuals around him, founded a famous colony of artists here.*

49

**Below:**
With one half convex and the other concave, the stairs at the art museum in Bonn have rightly been proclaimed an architectural masterpiece. Joining the foyer and rooms of exhibits, the construction is a real eye-catcher.

**Below centre:**
The new Design Centre of North Rhine-West-phalia in Essen used to be a mining company boiler house. English star architect Sir Norman Foster has managed to restore and convert the enormous complex to suit its new function in keeping with true Bauhaus tradition.

**Bottom:**
Essen was ruled by „canon king" Alfred Krupp. His Villa Hügel, built in the Ruhr hills near Brederney from plans he had drawn up himself, was made over to a public foundation in 1954, which since that date has used the building as a centre for the arts.

**Page 52/53:**
*Roofs of bluish-grey slate and gleaming white facades criss-crossed with dark wooden beams are the traits of the old part of Freudenberg in the Siegerland.*

**Below:**
*Shrouded in legend and the subject of many different interpretations, the Externsteine near Detmold dominate the eastern reaches of the Teutoburg Forest. This fabled cluster of rocks fascinates nature-lovers and mystics alike. The monoliths are known to have been an early place of heathen worship.*

**Above centre:**
*On the Lower Rhine at Xanten. The Rhine waterway was an important artery for the Romans who transported troops and goods along it. Their Colonia Ulpia Traiana later became Xanten.*

**Above:**
*The scenery along the Lower Rhine may not be as dramatic as that of the middle section of the river, yet it has its own persistent charm. Ancient meads have remained, such as those near the Bislich islands, preserving the river's authentic character and providing sanctuary for a number of plants and animals.*

For over 700 years the landscape of northern Germany was scattered with windmills, like the one here at Petershagen. Now very much a rarity, the creak of sails in the wind, turning heavy stones to grind the corn, is a thing of the past.

**Right:**
Even in the Middle Ages, Rhine metropolis Cologne was considered to be one of the largest and richest cities in the west. The development of both the town and its inhabitants has been guided by the river, whose floods have tested the patience and ingenuity of the people of Cologne for centuries. When the waters rise, the parts of town nearest the river (here the Alter Markt with the Romanesque church of St Martin's) can only be reached via makeshift footbridges.

**Below:**
Even though it's considerably shorter than the television tower, Cologne Cathedral is indisputably the city's local landmark. Following 600 years of building activity, the largest Gothic church in Germany wasn't completed until 1880. Its lavish interior reflects the significance and power the diocese held in the area.

**Right:**
For a taste of that proverbial, bubbling, Rhineland joie de vivre, come to Cologne or Düsseldorf during Carnival. The highlight of the silly season are the processions on Rosenmontag, the last Monday before Lent, when the whole town is out on the streets celebrating.

*The old diocesan town of Münster. The historic heart of the city is said to be one of the most beautiful in Germany. The Gothic town hall witnessed the signing of the Peace of Westphalia in 1648, which brought an end to the Thirty Years' War.*

*Raesfeld is not just one of the most resplendent moated castles in Westphalia, but also a place of great historical importance. During the Thirty Years' War, field marshal to the emperor, Count Alexander II von Velen, turned the estate into an imperial centre of politics and the arts.*

*Haus Bodelschwingh is another of the many moated strongholds distributed around the Westphalian countryside. Where there were no hills or mountains to offer natural protection, water was used as a method of defence.*

*Wuppertal, in the Bergisches Land, is a city with a long tradition and an extremely unusual form of transport. Its „futuristic" suspension railway was installed in 1900 by engineer Karl Eugen Langen. Although the public transport system is now a century old, it still glides between the houses. „It may be old iron", say the locals proudly, „but it's not rusty!"*

*The first of its kind in Germany, built between 1894 and 1899, the ship hoist at Henrichenburg on the Dortmund-Ems Canal was in operation until 1962. It was used to lift ships from one level of the canal to another. The subject of great engineering interest, the plant can be visited as part of the Westphalian Industrial Museum.*

*Known as the „musical corner" of the Saxon Vogtland, the Musik-winkel jutting into Bohemia has absorbed the musical traditions of its neighbour. Markneukirchen and the surrounding villages are home to a number of instrument makers, often sought out by great virtuosi commissioning them to built the perfect violin.*

Following the Reunification of Germany there was a lot of refreshing of geography to be done on both sides of the border. There was the wonderful architecture of the old Hanseatic towns of Rostock, Stralsund, Wismar and Greifswald to be discovered. Hymns of praise were composed for cobbled streets which elsewhere had been covered in tarmac, considered more suitable in the age of the automobile. The bone-shaking action of the suspension was a bit of nostalgia to be relished, as was the unique experience of passing under the leafy archways of ancient trees.

Today people are pretty familiar with both parts of Germany. They not only cherish the cobblestones but also the brand-new surfaces covering the many tourist trails devoted to a particular topic. One of these is the Silver Route which joins up the rich mountain towns of Saxony's Erzgebirge. During Advent, when snow dusts the fields and trees and carved decorations light up the windows, this effuses a very special atmosphere.

Those who prefer to travel on foot have also unearthed their own favourite bits of greater Germany. One destination which has attracted an especially large number is the Thuringian Forest and in particular its legendary mountain hiking route, the Rennsteig. First mentioned in 1330, its actual age is as much a mystery as why it exists at all. Along the 100-odd miles (168 kilometres) of the ridge you may not always be alone but you're always on top of the world. Literally. And, filled with a deep feeling of satisfaction and of being at peace with everyone and everything, also spiritually.

**Below:**
*Stralsund is one of the most delightful coastal towns in Mecklenburg-West Pomerania. Its joining of the Hanseatic League in 1293 heralded the start of a long period of ascendancy whose architectural heritage includes over 400 listed properties. Stralsund is also where the 1936 road and rail dam to Rügen starts out from.*

**Right:**
*Caspar David Friedrich, the famous Romantic artist, often chose the ruined Eldena monastery near his native Greifswald as the subject of his paintings. The former Cistercian abbey was founded in 1199 and played a leading role in converting West Pomerania to Christianity.*

**Left:**
Rostock, with a population of a quarter of a million, lies sheltered on the Warnow estuary on the Baltic Sea. Slavs were early settlers here, banished by the arrival of new colonists in c. 1200.

Work on St Mary's, which rises up above everything in its vicinity, began in c. 1230. The mighty church was completed in 1452.

**Below:**
View of the old harbour of Wismar with the Schabelthaus, which was the house of the mayor. The Wassertor, an imposing 15th-century brick gateway, was once part of the city defences.

**Above centre:**
The Nikolaikirche towers up above the patrician houses in the foreground with their elaborate façades. One of the features of the interior is the Gothic „seaman's altar".

**Above:**
Greifswald, also a Hanseatic city, is rich in historical buildings. Places to visit include the cathedral, Marienkirche, the courtyard of the St Spiritus hospital and also the decorative

gabled houses lining the market place. The town hall, originally Gothic, was renovated in 1738 following a fire.

**Below:**
The island of Rügen is one of the most popular holiday resorts on the Baltic coast. The amount of water which has penetrated the land and vice versa is so great that no town or village is further than 5 miles (8 km) from the coast. The fishing village of Baabe (its beach is shown here) is one of the resorts which has only fairly recently joined the ranks of the spa towns.

**Right:**
Twin lighthouses on Kap Arkona. The smaller of the two was erected in the neo-Classical period and is the work of none other than famous Prussian architect Karl Friedrich Schinkel. From here it's a mere stone's throw to the much-admired chalk cliffs which drop down a sheer 164 ft (50 m) into the swirling sea.

**Far right:**
The restored pier in Sellin shines brightly once more. The fishing hamlet, nestling between the southern slopes of the Forthberg and Selliner See, was unheard of until 1895, when the first guests arrived here on the narrow-gauge railway.

**Below:**
The Kaiser Wilhelm Hotel and Villa Germania are just two of the buildings in Bansin which have finally awakened from a long, deep sleep. The much-frequented resort on the Baltic coast is in the east of Usedom and, like its neighbours Heringsdorf and Ahlbeck, has a fine sandy beach.

**Below centre and bottom:**
The first tourist to visit the little fishing village of Ahrenshoop on the Darß peninsula in 1880 was a painter. He couldn't have imagined in his wildest dreams that so many would follow him here. The artists' colony dates back to the turn of the 19th century and is still patronised by famous names in art and literature.

65

The spacious grounds and palace of Schloss Sanssouci in the old Prussian capital of Potsdam are an absolute must. In the middle of the 18th century,

King Friedrich II took the planning of this masterpiece of „Frederick the Great Rococo“ into his own hands, proving in the sumptuous palace interiors

and also in the gardens that he wasn't just a man of war but also one of artistic ability and stylish creativity

Following Germany's expansion eastwards, the first German city east of the Elbe was Schwerin, quickly becoming the seat of the local count in 1167 and a diocesan town in 1171. The residence of the dukes of Mecklenburg, preserved in all its finery, was modelled on Chambord in the Loire Valley and built between 1843 and 1857. The plans were provided by a number of famous contemporary architects, among them Gottfried Semper.

The new orangery at Sanssouci is the result of an artistic dream harboured by King Friedrich Wilhelm IV, an expression of Germanic longing for Italy. The orangery quotes buildings of the Italian Renaissance, one example being the Villa Medici in Rome, and was constructed from 1851 to 1857.

**Below centre:**
The leafy waterways between Lübbenau and Lehde are the roads of the Spree Forest, an area dominated by water. The unrivalled biotope of the Spree Delta is, however, slowly bursting at the seams. The flood of visitors wanting to be punted along the tree-covered canals in traditional flat-bottomed boats, at least, is proving too great for the region to cope with.

**Below:**
The little town of Werder, situated on an island in the River Havel, is known for its orchards and fruit wine. The blossom on the fruit trees is celebrated at a special festival here each May. In keeping with its local produce, the church has a wooden depiction of Christ pressing fruit.

Theodor Fontane is the poet of the Mark Brandenburg. There are still plenty who follow his „Walks through the Mark Brandenburg" which he notated in the travel journal of the same name. His native town of Neuruppin erected a monument to him in 1907.

Schloss Branitz lies just outside Cottbus. The building, embellished by Gottfried Semper, is girdled by an elegant park designed by the owner of the palace, Prince Hermann Pückler. The famous landscape gardener is laid to rest in his park in a pyramid of earth, surrounded by water.

**Page 70/71:**
The Quadriga, with Victoria at the reigns, surmounts the Brandenburg Gate in Berlin. Carried off to France by Napoleon, in 1814 the Prussians fetched their goddess of victory back home. In the background is the dome of the new Reichstag.

**Right:**
The Memorial Church to
Kaiser Wilhelm on
Breitscheidplatz was
built at the end of the
19th century and badly
damaged in the last
world war. The remains,
known as the „hollow
tooth", were integrated
into the new church, built
between 1959 and 1963.

**Below:**
Schloss Charlottenburg,
built by King Friedrich I
at the end of the 17th
century for his wife,
Charlotte, is the perfect
architectural embodi-
ment of the absolutist
Prussian conception of
the state.

**Left:**
In the 1920s Potsdamer Platz was one of the busiest squares in Europe. After it had existed in name alone for several decades, when the Wall came down it suddenly had the dubious honour of being the biggest building site on the Continent. The new heart of Berlin now has a new face to match.

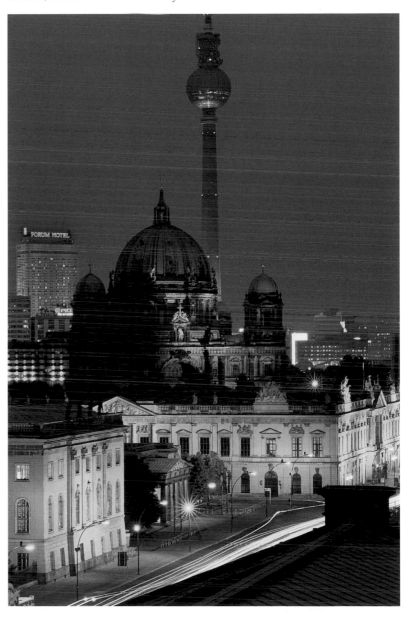

**Above:**
Perspectives old and new: Berlin Cathedral on Gendarmenmarkt once monopolised the city's historic silhouette. In its day, the television tower on Alexanderplatz was an object of prestige for the GDR.

**Left:**
The bizarre rock formations of the Elbsandsteingebirge, better known under the not inappropriate name of Saxon Switzerland, are a hot favourite with German and international tourists. The area was designated a national park on 1 October 1990.

**Left:**
With a vertical drop of ca. 650 ft (200 m) down to the Elbe, the Bastei Massif has one of the best panoramic views of the valley.

**Below:**
In 1825 a first wooden bridge was built linking the towering rocks of the Bastei. The stone bridge there today is from 1851. It leads through a rock archway to the 14th-century ruins of Neurathen Castle.

**Above:**
The walls of rock near Neurathen are both impressive and famous. Not far from the village of Rathen is an open-air stage, squeezed in beneath these colossal natural monuments.

**Below:**
On Dresden's Theaterplatz stands the famous opera house which bears the name of its equally renowned creator, Gottfried Semper. Built between 1871 and 1878, it was reopened in 1985 following an extensive programme of restoration.

**Left:**
Saxon elector and Polish king Friedrich August, whose strength earned him the title Augustus the Strong (he could bend a horseshoe with his bare hands), was the mastermind behind Dresden. In his „Venice of the East" the Elbe, like the Canal Grande, was the city's main artery, lined with magnificent buildings.

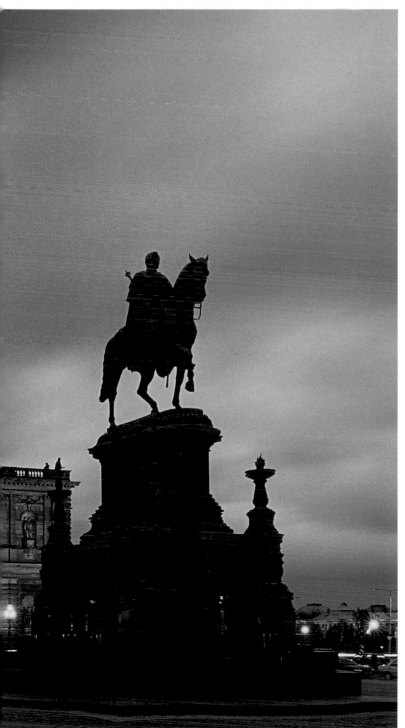

*Left:*
*Dresden's splendid baroque residential palace is the Zwinger, built by royal architect Matthäus Daniel Pöppelmann from 1711 to 1728. Its structure and valuable museum collections are impressive.*

***Above centre:***
*„This picture alone represents an entire artist's world", enthused Goethe on seeing Raphael's „Sistine Madonna", the most famous work of art at the Alte Meister gallery in the Dresden Zwinger. The collection, begun under Augustus the Strong, is one the world's most significant.*

***Above:***
*The Moritzburg hunting lodge in the Dresden green belt was also the work of patron Augustus and architect Pöppelmann. The palace, surrounded by a wonderful park, is a real tourist magnet. The lodge was named not after the man who completed but the one who began construction on it, Duke Moritz (1542–46).*

**Left:**
Leipzig's Nikolaikirche, the oldest and also largest house of worship in Leipzig, was the place of inception for the peaceful revolution of 1989. On 9 October, 70,000 people marched from the church through the middle of town, triggering the enormous social changes which then occurred in East Germany.

**Below:**
Leipzig's Himmelsfinger skyscraper is almost 500 ft (150 m) tall and part of the university. The Gewandhaus concert hall (left), home to the orchestra of the same name, squats contentedly beneath it, with the new opera house in the foreground.

**Above:**
The design of Leipzig's main station from 1915 proves that iron and glass need not necessarily be cold and rigid, but can be used artistically in playful animation. The station includes a shopping centre, which now straddles several floors.

Germany wouldn't be romantic Germany without its castles. Yet less than two hundred years ago many of these medieval strongholds lay in ruins, dynamited by their enemies or simply abandoned by their owners. The country, a motley collection of independent states, some quite tiny, was gripped by a similar, political lethargy. The concept of the strong nation state was either a dream for the future or an inaccurate memory of the past. The „rediscovered" Middle Ages was a far cry from the rose-coloured reconstructions dreamt up by 19th-century idealists. Knights in shining armour were often wolves in sheep's clothing. Yet the walls which had witnessed the past without the Romantic frills were to benefit from this utopianism. Crumbling fortresses

were suddenly very much in the public eye; some were rebuilt, often beyond recognition, and others were at least secured before they fell into further disrepair.

There are several „classic" areas of castles in Germany, the best-known being the Middle Rhine. The picturesque valley from Mainz to Koblenz, best seen from aboard a pleasure boat, is positively littered with fortresses. They have defensive names like Ehrenfels, Rheinstein, Gutenfels, Marksburg, Stolzenfels and Lahneck or, in one case, the feindliche Brüder („enemy brothers"). The most unusual is undoubtedly the one built like a stone ship in the middle of the Rhine, Pfalzgrafenstein or Pfalz near Kaub.

As one can guess, this poetic landscape does not have a peaceful origin. Down the centuries territories were guarded by castles on both sides of the old River Rhine border. A stronghold high up above the valley floor

was not only a mark of patriotism but also of financial surety. The tolls and other tributes paid by the sailors and merchants who passed by provided local castellans with a steady source of income.

The second heavily-castled river, the Saale, is in the east of Germany. Reference to its many fortified residences is made, among other places, in a famous song which proclaims: „On the white strands of the Saale stand castles proud and bold." In the 10th century the river was a national boundary, which separated Franks, Thuringians and Saxons on one side from Slavs on the other, until Saxon emperors wishing to extend their lands marched east. The smaller Saale can of course hardly compete with the mighty Rhine for size and impressiveness, yet it does have qualities of its own. It first meanders through the mountains and then swells out into two (artificial) lakes with a fjord-like shoreline. The castles themselves are just as old, historically interesting and romantic as their Rhineland counterparts. Schloss Burgk, for example, boasts the biggest kitchen fireplace in Germany and the heated chamber in Orlamünde is where the White Lady, Germany's most famous castle ghost, was first spotted. Other Saale fortresses well worth visiting are Burg Ranis, Heidecksburg, the ruins Rudelsburg and Saaleck and Giebichenstein near Halle. The unchallenged castle queen of the Saale Valley is Leuchtenburg near Kahla.

For a lot of castles within a relatively small area there's what is rather exuberantly known as Franconian Switzerland. The area between the towns of Bamberg, Erlangen

and Bayreuth has a multitude of valleys and hills which needed defending. This explains the prolific number of strong houses, with Auseß, Greifenstein, Egloffstein, Gößweinstein, Rabenstein and Pottenstein among them. From the air it looks as though some-

*Far left:*
The Wartburg above Eisenach has come to stand for the freedom and unity of Germany.

*Left:*
Schloss Mespelbrunn lies hidden away in the Spessart Forest.

# CASTLES

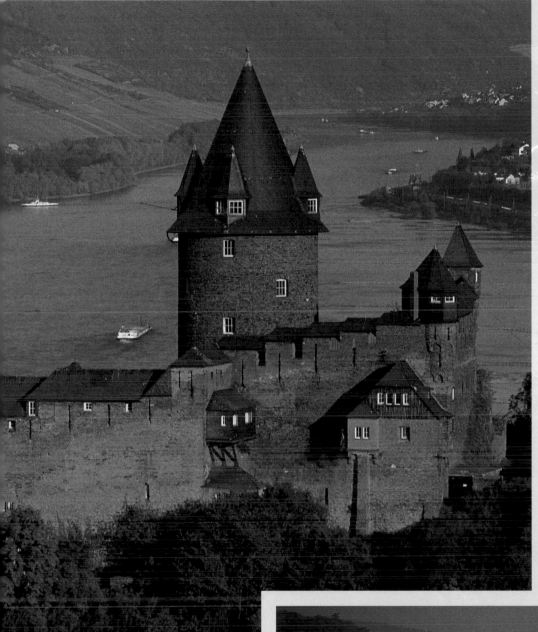

one has tipped a box of toys out onto the countryside, maybe belonging to a giant who liked to build castles and then violently smash them up...

It's quite understandable that with so many to choose from, selecting the most beautiful castle in Germany is not an easy task. This claim to fame must inevitably be shared by two top candidates. The first contender is Burg Eltz, the prototype medieval fairy-tale castle in the Eifel hills. Eight residential towers adorned with turrets and oriels make up a breath-taking, superlative whole. Joint first place in the superlative stakes goes to the Wartburg high up above Eisenach. In addition to its romantic appearance and setting, the Wartburg is also a symbol of cultural and historical significance for Germany.

**Above:**
*View of the Rhine. In the background is the legendary castle of Stahleck above Bacharach.*

**Above right:**
*Burg Eltz near the Moselle River is the prototype medieval castle.*

**Right:**
*Like a ship in a storm: the Pfalz at Kaub.*

**Page 82/83:**
The story goes that the Wartburg was founded in the 11th century. Legend also has it that in 1207 a minnesinger competition was held here. The six famous participants allegedly included Walther von der Vogelweide and Wolfram von Eschenbach. The loser, Heinrich von Ofterdingen, would have perished had he not been snatched from the clutches of death by the magician Klingsor.

**Left:**
The collegiate church of St Servatius on the castle hill in Quedlinburg is an 11th-century basilica. In the hall crypt of this striking Romanesque building Heinrich I, king of Saxony, and his wife Mathilde lie buried. The ancient cathedral jewels are particularly valuable.

**Below:**
Wernigerode goes back to the 10th century. Its citizens and local potentates worked in close collaboration to build up their home. The tremendous town hall from the end of the 15th century, for example, was erected on the foundations of the counts' Romanesque casino.

**Below:**
View of the market place in Wittenberg with a statue of Luther in the foreground and the mighty westwork of the Marienkirche where the Reformer preached. His famous theses, in which he attacked the indulgences of the papacy, were pinned to the door of the palace chapel.

**Below centre:**
Picturesque Finkenherd at the foot of the castle hill in Quedlinburg is said to be the place where Saxon Prince Heinrich was told he had been elected king of Germany. At the time he was indulging in his favourite pastime: catching birds.

**Above:**
In the west choir of Naumburg Cathedral visitors can study one of the most poignant artistic messages of the Romanesque. The stone figures of church patrons, the most famous of which bear the names Ekkehard and Uta, tell of a cold warrior and his beautiful, vulnerable wife.

85

*Time almost seems to have stood still in the Werdenfelser Land near Garmisch-Partenkirchen. This mountain farmer with his herd of young cows is the obvious symbol of a farming tradition which with all its customs and festivals has survived to the present day.*

The forest has played a major part in the mythology, history and economy of Germany. It thus comes as a surprise that the largest expanses of woodland are not in Bavaria or Thuringia, but in Hesse. It's believed that the Hessian Odenwald was the site of a number of stories in the „Song of the Nibelungen", that epic of early German literature. This is also where the babbling brook medieval hero Siegfried was murdered at is said to be.

Another area where natural sources are of great local significance is the north of Bavaria. Here, the ancient cathedral city of Bamberg and the formerly Prussian town of Kulmbach front Upper Franconia, world-famous for its beer. Nowhere else in Germany have the clear springs to supply so many breweries producing an unbelievable variety of beers. Many of the small, family-run businesses make both the beverage and the traditional bar food they serve in their establishments: bread baked in their own ovens, meat, sausage and ham from animals they slaughter themselves.

The topographical highlight of the south are the Alps, the highest being the Zugspitze at 9,721 feet (2,963 metres). Water sports fanatics can pursue their favourite line of activity on Lake Constance, Germany's largest inland waterhole whose shores are divided on the German side between Baden-Württemberg and Bavaria.

If this isn't enough and you want something really final, then it's not far to the „view of the end of the world" from here. For this you have to go to Baden, where the palace and gardens of Schloss Schwetzingen pay homage to the golden age of 18th-century Palatinate. Here, in a leafy fountain alcove, plants and paintings cleverly create the illusion that this is where the world comes to an end.

# TO THE ALPS

**Page 88/89:**
The pretty Moselle village of Cochem, ruled today by Bacchus, the god of wine, is of Celtoroman origin. The old imperial castle with its stalwart keep has guarded the bend in the river since the 11th century. The stronghold was later destroyed, only being rebuilt in its present form in the 19th century.

**Right above:**
It's a known fact that the Rhine and wine go well together. Bacharach, with a 1,000 years of history behind it, has long been said to produce a particularly good vintage. Its vineyards are offset by an extremely artistic backdrop, consisting of the ruined Wernerkapelle and the old Staufer fortress of Stahleck.

**Right:**
Ancient „golden" Mainz is the provincial capital of Rhineland-Pfalz and a diocesan and university town. The Romans made the settlement at the confluence of Main and Rhine the capital of their Germania Superior province. In c. 1450 Gutenberg invented the art of printing books here. Mainz's main attraction is the Romanesque cathedral, whose construction spanned nine centuries.

**Right below:**
Going to Trier, the oldest city in Germany, is like being transported back to the days of the Romans, with their basilica, ancient Moselle bridge, the remains of the baths and amphitheatre. The absolute highlight is the Porta Nigra in the heart of town, the north gate and largest surviving Roman arch in the world.

**Right:** The abundance of castles on the Middle Rhine is legendary. Wherever you look there are medieval fortresses, some as majestic ruins on rocky outcrops, others in the middle of the river, like the Pfalzgrafenstein at Kaub.

# THE LAND

SFrom time immemorial, Bacchus and Gambrinus have been wrestling for favouritism among the people of Germany. To be more exact, it's not actually the gods themselves who are engaged in healthy competition, but the beverages they represent: wine and beer. Wine was probably the first of the two to be planted in Germany and also the one to suffer a terrible catastrophe in the 19th century, when the vineyards were almost completely decimated by the dreaded vine pest. Since then, cultivation of the grape has been on a much smaller scale.

In more recent times, a striving for quality among a number of young vintners has earned wine from Germany a good re-

putation. New methods in the growing and processing of wine and the limiting of the yield per hectare have in the past few years proved successful. Riesling from the Rheingau and Moselle-Saar-Ruwer area enjoys international acclaim; red Spätburgunder from Baden or the Palatinate, which used to be called „liquid jam", need no longer shun comparison with its French neighbours. This new self-confidence has also traversed to the elevated spheres of state receptions, where guests of the Bundesregierung are handed glasses of wine from Germany and nowhere else.

Many locals and tourists not only cherish the drink itself but also the ancient landscapes sculpted by centuries of viniculture. The atmospheric little wine villages are

**Left:**
*All hands on deck for the grape harvest!*

**Above:**
*In the Markgräflerland rolling hills mark the transition from Rhine plateau to Black Forest. In this area blessed with plenty of sunshine – here with Ballrechten in the background – viniculture is tradition.*

**Above right:**
*The discerning look of the vintner, checking the colour of a young wine.*

particularly popular during the grape harvest in autumn, when people come together to celebrate the new wine and – amid much merriment – themselves and their friends.

Germany's winelands are the northernmost contained areas of vineyard in the world. Consequently, the period of vegetation is comparatively short and the weather (frost in spring and autumn, the cold in winter, periods of rain or drought in the summer) poses a great problem. For this reason vines are only grown on the flat in Rheinhessen and Rhine Palatinate; they otherwise adorn

sunny ranges of hills and precipitous slopes facing southeast to southwest.

The largest area of cultivation (Germany's „chamber of wine") is Rhine Palatinate. The forests of the Palatinate, the Vosges and the Haardt boast an almost Mediterranean climate which produces hearty, light, sweet wines. The region stretches from Schweigen on the Alsatian border to the gates of Worms. The picturesque towns and villages of Bergzabern, Edenkoben, Hambach, Dürkheim (Germany's biggest wine-growing community), Herzheim and Bockenheim are linked by the German Wine Route.

Northerly Rheinhessen produces sweet, lively, fragrant vintages. Famous dramatist Carl Zuckmayer not inappropriately described his homeland's native tipple as „laughing wine". Among the best-known vintner villages in Rheinhessen are Alsheim, Oppenheim, Nierstein, Ingelheim – and Bingen. It's no great coincidence that mystic and Benedictine abbess Hildegard of Bingen (1098–1179) prescribed wine for medicinal purposes. Legend even has it that she once saved the area from the plague with the juice of the grape.

Wonderful tales of wine-cum-magic potion are also common to Franconia, whose areas of vineyards surrounding the city of Würzburg were much bigger in the Middle Ages than they are now. What hasn't changed is the high standard of Franconia's wine and a local dictum which claims that it can „heal the sick". So that there's no mistaking the curative, it comes in special round flagons with a name which in itself smacks of witches and bubbling cauldrons: „pouch of buck" (Bocksbeutel).

Yet the area which grandly claims to be the „hub of German wine culture" is not any of those already mentioned. Nor is it one of the no less prominent regions of Baden-Württemberg, the rivers of the Nahe, Moselle, Saar, Ruwer and Ahr nor the tiny Middle Rhine with Bacharach and all the others. Germany's number one in wine is the Rheingau. The spectrum of admirers and patrons of its alcoholic refreshment ranges from the Romans to Charlemagne, from the Cistercians at the monastery in Eberbach to the Benedictines on Johannisberg, from Goethe to Queen Victoria. The queen indeed was a particular fan of bottles from Hochheim, bequeathing to the English-speaking world the word „hock" as a general designation for wine from the area.

There are also two minute wine-growing areas in the east of Germany. Vines thrive along the River Elbe near Meißen and at the confluence of Unstrut and Saale – and they're not the worst of vintages either...

*Far right:*
Wine cellars often have some real treasures stashed away in their vaults.

*Bottom right:*
A lot of hard work is necessary before the grape becomes juice.

**Right:**

Even if its contemporary skyline suggests quite the opposite, the city of Frankfurt is over 1,200 years old. Frankfurt is the birthplace of Goethe and of civic parliamentarianism, instigated in 1848 almost 100 years after Goethe's birth at the Paulskirche national assembly.

**Top:**

Wiesbaden, the capital of Hesse, lies at the base of the Taunus Mountains. The healing waters of the Roman spa, which in the 19th century made the town one of the most luxurious health resorts in Europe, still bubble up from the ground. The state theatre of Hesse is from this period.

**Above:**

The Moselle flows into the Rhine at the Deutsches Eck in Koblenz. From here the two rivers branch off into some of the most wonderful valley scenery in Germany. The town itself has much to offer: a medieval city centre which goes back to the Romans, old churches and the popular Burg Rittersturz.

**Page 96/97:**
View of Freiburg from Lorettoberg. The church steeple, „the most beautiful tower in the Christian world", as historian Jakob Burkhardt put it, climbs 377 ft/115 m up into the sky and is visible for miles. The belfry is part of the famous minster Unserer Lieben Frau, on which building was begun in c. 1200.

**Above:**
One of the oldest country open-air museums is the Vogtsbauernhof, named after one of its buildings, in Gutach in the Black Forest. The museum has various types of houses, country crafts and gardens on display, not forgetting the distillery where the Black Forest's beloved Obstler schnapps is made.

**Right:**
With the gardening done, it's time for a sit-down on the old wooden bench to contemplate the day's work and future plans. The people of the Black Forest may be considered industrious, but they also know how to enjoy life.

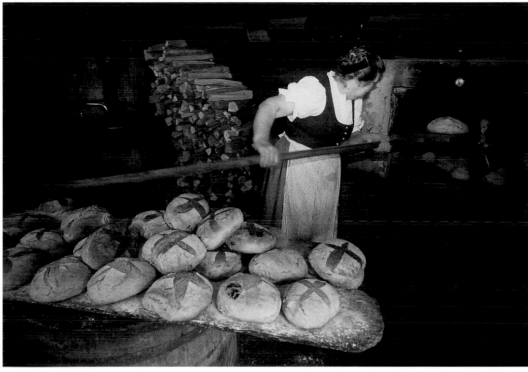

**Left:**
*Even if it takes a lot of time and effort, bread here is still home-baked on a daily basis according to the old custom. Local bakers swear that not only do their loaves taste better and have more flavour, but also that they keep longer.*

**Below:**
*A harmonious unison of hills and valleys, of field and forest, of nature and mankind such as this can be found in the Middle Black Forest, near Landwasser in the Oberprechtal, an offshoot of the Elz Valley.*

**Left:**
The venue is the old free city of Rottweil, the date Rosenmontag, eight o'clock in the morning, the event the Narrensprung, the procession of fools, one of the most popular of Swabia's Alemannic Carnival. For many in the Black Forest and its neighbouring areas, such as in the ancient ecclesiastical territories along Lake Constance, this is the fifth season of the year.

**Below:**
Fasnet traditions date from way back when, as do the wooden masks and costumes. Devils, witches, demons and other ghoulish figures rattle noisily through the streets, driving out winter in anticipation of spring. The proceedings call for plenty of Carnival pranks, cunning and clamorous merriment.

**Above:**
At the stronghold of Carnival tradition in Elzach the eerie figures parade after dark. Lights illuminate the ghostly scene, which is enough to unnerve even the most stalwart of spectators. As opposed to Carnival in the Rhineland, Swabia's Alemannic version is darker, older – and far less adulterated.

**Below:**
The castle in Meersburg is the oldest inhabited fortress in Germany. Its history goes back to the 7th century. The rooms open to the public include the chamber Annette von Droste-Hülshoff worked and died in. In the 19th century, the female poet was one of the first to penetrate the then male world of literature.

**Right:**
One of the many high points along the German shore of Lake Constance is the pilgrimage church of Birnau, built by the nearby Cistercian monastery at Salem in extravagant Rococo in c. 1750.

**Centre right:**
The mild, sunny climate of Lake Constance provided the ideal conditions for Count Lennart Bernadotte to energetically put his idea into practice – that of turning the island belonging to Teutonic Order of Knights into a floral paradise surrounded by water. Mainau's carpets of blooms can be admired from April to October, with some of the hothouses open throughout the winter.

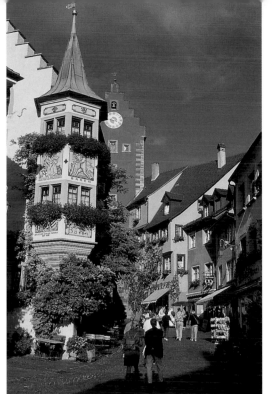

*If you go to Meersburg, dont just visit the castle. A stroll along the shores of the lake or a trek up through the steep narrow streets of the old town are just as rewarding. The hotchpotch of architectural styles ranges from Gothic and Renaissance to baroque and Biedermeier. The Obertor with the Hotel Bären oriel is just one of the many photogenic spots.*

*Above centre:*
*Radolfzell on the Mettnau peninsula has not one but three patron saints: Theopontus, Senesius and Zeno. Each year on the third Sunday in July a festival procession through the old*

*town is held in their honour. The following day, Hausherrenmontag, the people of Moos row across the Zeller See in boats adorned with flowers.*

*Above:*
*View of Überlingen from Wallhausen across Lake Constance. The old free city is a place of nostalgia and gourmet restaurants.*

**Left:**
The late baroque Neues Schloss in Stuttgart from the 18th century was commissioned by Duke Karl Eugen. The jubilee pillar on the palace square was erected in celebration of King Wilhelm I's silver jubilee in 1841.

**Below:**
As early as just after the First World War Stuttgart was seen as a bastion of modern architecture, its name inextricably linked to those of Walter Gropius, Le Corbusier and Mies van der Rohe. As the state capital of Baden-Württemberg, it obviously feels obliged to live up to its reputation. The Staatsgalerie building by James Stirling from 1984, for example, could thus be thought of as the prototype of the postmodern era in Germany.

**Above:**
Schloss Ludwigsburg has 452 rooms and was constructed at the beginning of the 18th century in answer to Versailles. The baroque gardens, which lack none of the elegance and grandeur of the palace, are a big pull, drawing millions of tourists a year.

Bamberg, the old imperial city and diocesan town in Franconia, is definitely in the top ten of beautiful German cities. The historic centre with its famous cathedral and colourful town hall in the middle of the Regnitz River is a UNESCO World Heritage Site.

**Below:**
Regensburg on the Danube was a place both the Romans and later Germany's kings and princes felt was worth settling in. The Romans built a castle here, with their successors holding Imperial Diets in the city. The stone bridge is 12th-century and the cathedral, which is dedicated to St Peter, is Gothic.

**Above centre:**
Nuremberg, capital of the Franconian region, was for centuries one of the political and intellectual centres of the empire. The photo depicts the intricate gable of the Frauenkirche. Each day at noon, seven electors trot round Emperor Karl IV while musicians play their instruments, a feature installed in 1509.

**Above:**
From a balcony on the Frauenkirche, each year at the start of Advent the Christ Child declares the most famous of Germany's Christmas fairs open. The hunt for Christmas presents is then on, interrupted only by the occasional glass of mulled wine or spicy Nuremberg sausage.

*Page 108/109:*
*Munich. View from St Peter's, the oldest church in the city, of Marienplatz at the heart of town. Whereas the new town hall has disguised its real age* *(despite its Gothic appearance, it's only 19th- and 20th-century), the twin domes of the Frauenkirche, Munich's local landmark, are half a millennium old.*

*Munich's Oktoberfest is a festival of superlatives; it's the biggest in the world! Here you can try out the newest and flashiest rides in the fairground business and also taste some of the local cuisine. The top victual is, of course,* *beer, which in the local vernacular is also referred to as „staple food-stuff no. 1". It's served in the traditional litre jugs, with the obligatory oompah band puffing away in the background as you sip.*

**Below and right:**
Munich's Englischer Garten runs 3 miles (5 km) along the Isar River over a breadth of about _ a mile (1 km). This makes it one of the largest inner-city parks in the world. When the weather's fine, half of Munich can be found here taking a walk, lying in the sun or firmly ensconced in one of the beer gardens. The Monopterus (below) is one of the many architectural decorations dotted about the gardens.

**Centre right:**
The beer garden is cultural heritage in Bavaria, and nowhere more so than in Munich. Friends meet under huge shady trees to drink beer and eat Weißwurst sausages, to watch people watching them. And if you think this honourable pastime is reserved for the height of summer, then think again! The first rays of sunshine, even if they are in January, herald the start of the beer garden

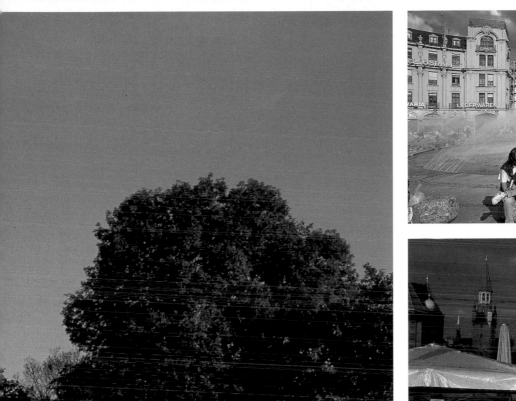

**Below:**
Karlsplatz, known locally as the Stachus, was once one of the busiest crossroads in town. It's now been pedestrianised, its fountains providing cool relief on hot summer days.

**Below centre:**
Viktualienmarkt, Munich's food market, does its name full justice. Here you can buy the best, freshest produce, most of it straight from the farmer. There are still some of those celebrated stallholders left, tough, weather-beaten souls who serve their customers with that special keen Munich wit. On the left of the picture is the old town hall, to the right the Heilig-Geist-Kirche.

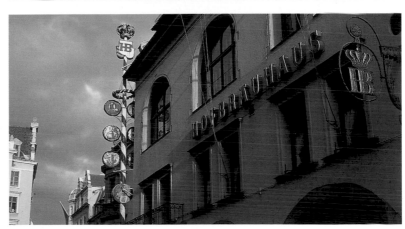

**Above:**
Out of the many famous beer temples in Munich, the cult Hofbräuhaus has just got to be number 1. Here you can drink, eat and sway along to the brewery hit „In Munich there's the Hofbräuhaus..."

Andechs Monastery bathed in morning sunshine on the shores of the Ammersee. Founded in 1460 by Duke Albrecht III of Bavaria, it later became an eminent place of pilgrimage. The Benedictines pro-vide fortification for both the mind and the body, the latter in the form of strong Andechs beer which the monks brew from an ancient recipe.

**Top:**
*The deep, moving sense of religiousness shared by the people of Bavaria is evident in the many wayside shrines and crosses spread about the countryside, such as the one here in Aidenried in the Pfaffenwinkel area.*

**Above and above centre:**
*The Wieskirche between Schongau and Füssen in the Allgäu is a masterpiece of southern German Rococo. The interior, absolutely smothered in stucco ornamentation and colourful frescos, is a feast for the eyes. When a military plane out training flew too close to the church, causing the walls to vibrate and the stucco to collapse, there was total dismay. The place of pilgrimage has since been restored to its former glory.*

# LUDWIG II OF BAVARIA

*Schloss Neuschwanstein rises up above the precipitous gorge of the Pöllatschlucht.*

For someone known as The Dream King of 19th-century Germany, it is appropriate that his castles look like something out of a fairy tale. In our prosaic, modern world, Ludwig II and Neuschwanstein, Linderhof and Herrenchiemsee still hold all the magic of a bygone age, drawing millions of tourists each year from all over the globe to Upper Bavaria.

King Ludwig II of Bavaria, son of Crown Prince Maximilian of Bavaria and his Prussian princess wife, was born in 1845. Following the early death of his father, Ludwig was made head of government at the tender age of 18, forced to function in an environment he abhorred. Despite his revulsion, he made an effort to be successful in his new role. His endeavours were recognised in 1883, three years before his mysterious death, by none other than the Prussian Imperial Chancellor Bismarck, who conceded that the king ruled „better than all his ministers". High praise indeed – which had a certain irony to it. Prussia's hegemonic politics and its two wars were something the sensitive Ludwig absolutely detested. He confided his misgivings to his dear friend Richard Wagner, dreading he would become „a puppet king without any power". Things in fact turned out worse than he feared; at the order of Germany's princes, Ludwig had to offer the imperial crown to his private adversary, the king of Prussia.

These crass realities would probably have been the end of Ludwig if he hadn't found escape in another, fairy tale world, a world where he made all the rules and could be

**Above left:**
*The mirrored gallery at Herrenchiemsee is even bigger than the French original.*

**Left:**
*For Ludwig II, Schloss Hohenschwangau up above the Alpsee was „paradise on earth".*

# AND HIS CASTLES

king as he saw fit. The Bavarian monarch was a great admirer of the French Sun King Louis XIV. Yet in his desire to honour the obligations of their shared name, he sadly failed to acknowledge that in the one-and-a-half centuries which separated him from the French regent, much had changed. The rest is history. In an attempt to make his wildest dreams come true – that of a poetic existence à la Lohengrin, Tristan and Tannhäuser – he soon found himself in dire financial straits. He grossly underestimated the capacities of the royal coffers, which for a Bavarian king of the bourgeois 19th century were far more modest that those of the absolutist French sovereign. Ludwig's castles swallowed up his money at an incredible rate. Accused of bringing the country to ruin, he was deemed an incurable madman and certified. On 13 June 1886, the ill-fated ruler and his psychiatrist were found drowned in the Starnberger See.

Ludwig's bequest to us are his castles. Ruined Hohenschwangau, for example, was initially scheduled for renovation only; it was to be turned into a humble baronial abode. Ludwig's original plans were soon abandoned, however, in favour of designs for a romantic four-storey edifice on a monumental scale. In his mind's eye was a Bavarian version of the palace at the gigantic Wartburg in Eisenach. The king even travelled incognito to Thuringia to see the castle for himself and gain inspiration. Yet time was not on his side. When he died, only part of his dream home of Neuschwanstein was finished. The rest was completed posthumously in accordance with his wishes and ideas.

In comparison with this fantastic construction set against its bizarre Alpine backdrop, Schloss Linderhof seems extremely unassuming and private. And the park, too, with its contrived Venus Grotto, Moroccan House and Oriental Pavilion, symbolises more a personal preoccupation of the king with foreign myths and cultures rather than

something public. Once the monarch had glided through the palace gates in his golden Rococo sledge he was alone, with only his staff to bother him. Linderhof was incidentally the only one of his building projects he saw completed.

His third castle, Schloss Herrenchiemsee on Chiemsee lake, was to be a „new Versailles". In 1878 the foundations were laid for a huge building whose main façade actually trumped that of the prototype. The king, who usually only came to his island palace at night, attached great importance to detail, insisting that the furnishings be copied from the French originals. While Paul Verlaine celebrated the regent as the „last true king of this century", others angrily called him a mad squanderer. Ludwig, in his own words, claimed to be neither, professing to „remain an eternal puzzle".

**Richard Wagner** (right) **in a letter** (1866) **about Ludwig II:**

„I persistently consider the young King Ludwig to be immensely competent. Yet how his qualities of leadership shall develop remains to be seen. An inconceivably futile education has succeeded in arousing in the young man a deep-seated aversion to earnest preoccupation with state interests which to date shows absolutely no sign of abating. He performs matters of state ... full of loathing. He is disgusted by his family, by the entire court indeed; he hates the army and soldiery; he finds the aristocracy ridiculous and his subjects contemptible. Yet about the clergy he expresses himself clearly and without prejudice; on matters of religion he is serious and ardent."

*Above far right:*
*Schloss Herrenchiemsee was modelled on Versailles.*

*Above right:*
*Schloss Linderhof, the smallest of Ludwig II's palaces, was the only one he actually lived in.*

**Below and below centre:**
In Bavaria, St Leonhard has long been the patron saint of animals. On 6 November, his name day, Leonhard processions are staged in many of the villages, such as here in Fischhausen on the Schliersee (below) and in Harmating near Bad Tölz (below centre). The parade culminates in the participants riding splendidly adorned horses and horse-drawn carts around the churches and chapels to be blessed by the priest.

**Above:**
The mountain hunting festival in Lenggries is a high point of the year for locals and visitors alike. This is when the hunters – in full traditional dress – choose their king. Once the ceremony is over, the rest of the night is spent drinking beer, eating hearty plates of food and dancing to the strains of Bavarian folk music.

In Upper Bavaria many ancient customs have been preserved. People not only dress up for church on Sundays but also for pilgrimages, donning their local costumes as a matter of course and not for the tourists.

**Left page:**
The parish church of
St Fabian and Sebastian
in Ramsau in the
Berchtesgadener Land is
a renowned Alpine motif.
Further features include
some very artistic carv-
ing on the gallery and
also the old cemetery
with graveyard crosses
from the 17th and 18th
centuries.

**Left:**
The Königssee is the
pearl of the Berchtesga-
dener Land. The grey
limestone rocks, some of
them up to 8,860 ft
(2,700 m) tall, are re-
flected in the dark green
water. Along its shores is
the old pilgrimage church
of St Bartholomä, dedi-
cated to St Bartholomew,
after whom the lake used
to be named.

On a clear day, from the
top of the Zugspitze,
Germany's highest
mountain, you have an
Alpine panorama spread
out beneath you.

121

# INDEX

Index...............Text..............Picture  Index...............Text..............Picture  Index...............Text..............Picture

*Typically Bavarian:*
*Hotel Post in Wallgau*
*near Mittenwald.*

## Credits

**Photos:**
*Günter Franz:*
p. 35 bottom.
*Jürgen Henkelmann:*
p. 16/17, 18/19, 66, 70/71, 73 top.
*Werner Richner:*
p. 80/81 top centre, 81 bottom right, 90 top left,
90 centre left, 91.
*Martin Siepmann:*
Front jacket, p. 5, 20/21, 86/87, 108/109, 110,
111 bottom right, 112-115 (10 ill.), 116 top left,
116 bottom right, 117 centre left, 117 top right,
118-124 (8 ill.).
*Karl-Heinz Raach:*
p. 10/11, 92/93 (5 ill.), 96-99 (5 ill.), 103 top left,
103 top right, 103 centre right, 103 bottom right.
*Publisher's archives:*
p. 117 bottom right (2 ill.).
*Horst und Daniel Zielske:*
p. 6/7, 8/9, 12/13, 14/15, 22-33 (25 ill.), 34, 35 top,
36-65 (64 ill.), 67 top, 67 bottom, 68/69, 72 bottom,
72 top, 73 right, 74-79 (12 ill.), 80 top left,
80 bottom right, 81 top right, 82-85 (6 ill.), 88/89,
90 bottom left, 94/95 (3 ill.), 100/101 (3 ill.),
102 bottom, 102 top, 104-107 (7 ill.), 111 top right,
116/117 top centre, back jacket.

**Design:**
hoyerdesign grafik gmbh, Freiburg

**Map:**
Fischer Kartografie, Fürstenfeldbruck

**Translation:**
Ruth Chitty, Schweppenhausen

Die Deutsche Bibliothek – CIP catalogue record
Journey through Germany / Ernst-Otto Luthardt
(author). – Würzburg: Verlagshaus Würzburg, 2000
ISBN 3-8003-0974-2

Printed in Germany
Reproductions by Artilitho, Trento
Printed by Konkordia Druck GmbH, Brühl
Bound by Josef Spinner Großbuchbinderei GmbH,
Ottersweier
© 2000 Verlagshaus Würzburg GmbH & Co. KG

ISBN 3-8003-0974-2